African
Elegance

African Elegance

ALICE MERTENS PHOTOGRAPHS

JOAN BROSTER TEXT

STRUIK PUBLISHERS

First published by
Purnell & Sons (S.A.) (Pty) Ltd

This edition published by
C. Struik Publishers (Pty) Ltd
Struik House, Oswald Pirow Street
Foreshore, Cape Town 8001.

1st Impression 1973 (Purnell)
2nd Impression 1979 (Purnell)
2nd Edition 1987 (Struik)

© Alice Mertons and Joan Broster 1973

Printed and bound by
Tien Wah Press (Pte) Ltd, Singapore

ISBN 0 86977 565 0

Contents

Introduction to Photographs

Bibliography

Burton, A.W.:
SPARKS FROM THE BORDER ANVIL
Provincial Publishers, 1950.

Holt, Basil:
WHERE RAINBIRDS CALL
Howard Timmins, 1972.

Hunter, Monica:
REACTION TO CONQUEST
Oxford University Press, 1936.

Macquarrie, J.W. (Edited by):
STANFORD'S REMINISCENCES, Volume One
Van Riebeeck Society, 1958.

Macquarrie, J.W. (Edited by):
STANFORD'S REMINISCENCES, Volume Two
Van Riebeeck Society, 1962.

Soga, J.H.:
THE AMAXOSA LIFE AND CUSTOMS
Lovedale Press, 1932.

Soga, J.H.:
THE SOUTH-EASTERN BANTU
Johannesburg, 1930.

Van Warmelo, N.J.:
A PRELIMINARY SURVEY OF THE BANTU TRIBES OF
SOUTH AFRICA
Government Printer, Pretoria, 1935.

Acknowledgements

We wish to thank the many people who helped to make this publication possible.

Our thanks go to the Government officials in the Transkei and in particular to Mr Hans Abraham, the Commissioner-General.

We also wish to thank the following friends for kindness, help, information and hospitality:—

Dr Enid Atkinson

Mr and Mrs Len Bode

Mr and Mrs Frank Daniel

Mr Dave Devitt

Mr Koos Erasmus and his son André

Mr David Ewels

Mr John Harrison

Mr and Mrs W. Heath

Mrs Stella McDonald

Miss N. Mgudlwa

Mr and Mrs Chris Pretorius

Mr and Mrs Leon Wood

Mrs N. Poswayo

Mr and Mrs C. Saliwa

Mrs A. Wishart and many others

Prologue

The aim of this book is to describe in photographs and words the beauty of the tribal people of the Transkei. Caught between western civilisation and ancient tribal life their beauty is a subject filled with poignancy, for the traditional way of life with its songs and dances is vanishing. The national dress, the colourful beadwork and the old customs are fast disappearing. In certain areas pitifully little remains. Nevertheless in most tribes costumes and customs are to be found. These we sought out and recorded. Their unique beauty, individuality and elegance are the subjects of our photographs.

It was a matter of urgency that we capture this life before it vanished. Therefore we chose from tribes where the traditional way of life had been retained. In all eight tribes, the Tembu, Gcaleka, Pondo, Bomvana, Mpondomise, Fingo, Bhaca and Xesibe, were photographed.

Our task was greatly facilitated by the help given to us by old traders and members of pioneering families. It was indeed fortunate that I belong to such a family. My father's family has lived in the Transkei for one hundred years. In 1875 my grandfather moved from Fingoland to Tembuland. Thus throughout the Transkei I have many relatives and close family friends. For generations these men and women have worked among the Africans and earned their love and confidence. It was to these friends and relatives that I appealed for assistance. They responded most generously and without their help we would not have succeeded. In each area they knew not only where the tribal life was to be found but also the individual families concerned. They introduced us and explained why we wished to take photographs. As a result we were made welcome and our presence accepted.

Thus we enjoyed surprising interludes of gay tribal life. Beadwork, songs and dances lit the scene. The magnificent and alluring tribal dress lends itself beautifully to documentaries and photographs. Writing alone cannot do justice to the elegance of the tribal people. The simplest turban is worn with style and distinction and every gesture is pleasing. As they lift a hand or wrap a blanket, tapered fingers shape the air with grace. All walk with inherent ease and quite naturally relax in exquisite positions.

Being indigenous people of Africa they have for centuries identified themselves with their surroundings and are deeply contained in its ancient rhythm. Without conscious effort they are charged with its reality and beauty, and with sure instinct grace the scene.

They are a warm-hearted and candid people. They have clear, melodious voices; speak vividly, fluently and with a great variety of tone and gesture. Their national tongue, Xhosa, has a natural flexibility and rhythm that is enhanced by the timbre of the African voice and the listening habits of the African ear.

All are masters of the arts of singing, dancing and comedy. As well as their own brand of disarming charm, they possess the poise and presence of stage celebrities. Like actors they hold the stage, and their fellow actors are as rapt as their audience. In their exuberant zest for life there is a mysterious attractiveness and power that is creative and vital.

DISTRIBUTION OF TRIBES

(IN TERMS OF MAIN CONCENTRATIONS)

CHAPTER I

A BEAUTIFUL LAND

*W*hen the visitor in southern Africa crosses the Great Kei River he enters a beautiful land. Ahead of him stretches the Transkei, the home of various Xhosa-speaking peoples. This territory, which is larger than Belgium, is bounded in the west by the high Drakensberg Mountains and in the east by the Indian Ocean. It is a well-watered land with many permanent rivers and its scenic beauty is unparalleled. High mountains, deep valleys, steep cliffs, waterfalls on winding rivers and undulating hills roll down to a rugged coastline. In this entrancing and untrammelled land live 4 000 000 Africans. The majority are peasant farmers and many still cling to the old tribal system and their ancient way of life.

On the hillsides herdboys tend cattle, sheep and goats, while in the mealie fields that dot the landscape like a patchwork, women hoe the lands. And everywhere are the round huts, neatly but distinctively thatched with thick grass. They are built of the dull grey-brown earth upon which they stand. The walls, approximately two metres high and 4½ metres in diameter, are patterned with white clay. The huts have a compactness of construction, size and proportion that is very pleasing to look upon. Their symmetry blends with the country. They look so much part of the scene that they appear to have grown out of the earth.

Each family resides in a group of these huts, known as a kraal. Each kraal consists of one or more huts, a cattlefold or byre, and a small garden lot. Life is patriarchal and in every kraal a man lives with his wives and children, together with his married sons and their wives and children. Each wife has her own hut but the first wife to be married is housed in a hut known as the Great House. The second wife lives in a hut called the Right-Hand House. The huts face east and are usually built in an arc with the cattlefold in the centre. The cattlefold is of the greatest significance, for cattle, sheep and goats play an important role in the social and ritual life. A man counts his wealth in cattle. His wives and daughters are valuable assets, for their bride price is always paid in cattle.

The whole structure of family life rests upon the worshipping of ancestral spirits. The ancestral belief, a primitive religion, is the very heart of the people and in it their culture is fused and set. On all solemn occasions of family life — at birth, initiation, marriage, death, seed time and harvest time, a propitiatory sacrifice is made to the ancestral spirits and it is followed by the appropriate songs and dances. All members of the family are required to attend this ceremony.

The head of the kraal acts as the officiating priest. He enters the cattlefold where, assisted by his sons or nephews, he sacrifices an ox, sheep or goat. As he sacrifices the·

animal he prays in a loud voice to his ancestral spirits, communicating the family's need. The spirits of the departed have power over only their own particular family. They control everything pertaining to this family. Rain, crops, cattle, wives, children, health and happiness are their bounty. They reward good and punish evil. The spirits of departed chiefs are the custodians of the tribe. They hold the destinies of their tribes in their keeping and exercise enormous influence. Sacrifices to them are offered by the tribal priests.

Throughout every sacrifice strict ritual is observed, for any neglect or misdemeanour would incur fiery wrath and retribution from the spirits. The people believe that when the animal is sacrificed, its cry calls to the ancestral spirits whereupon they return immediately to the precincts of the cattlefold. It is their sacred place and for this reason no woman, except in very special circumstances, is permitted to enter the cattlefold.

During the sacrifice the members of the family assemble in the space between the cattlefold and the huts. There, attired in their best, adorned in beadwork and paint, they greet their ancestors with song and dance. In the brightness of their rejoicing, the women and girls clap their hands to accentuate the beat and all stamp their feet. The songs of praise and worship belong to a set liturgy and everyone by some deep movement of life is drawn into the dance. In a mystical participation of Being, bodies sway and feet move ceaselessly in rhythm. This sound of dancing and singing, and the pageant of beauty, is very pleasing to the ancestral spirits who thenceforth guide and prosper the members of the family.

Later, according to strict convention, the various parts of the carcass are apportioned to the men, boys, women and children. When they have cooked their meat, beer is served and all partake of the sacrificial meat. After the feast the bones of the animal are burnt in the cattlefold but the skull and horns are placed on the gate-post. In the case of an illness where a witchdoctor has been called in, and an animal has been sacrificed, the skull and the horns are placed above the doorway of the patient's hut.

Beautiful tribal dress, beadwork, songs and dances are the media employed in ancestral worship but in everyday life those who adhere to this faith are recognised by the red ochre or clay which they apply to body, blankets and clothing. This is the colour of their faith and they are therefore called 'Red People'. The colour varies from the palest orange to the deepest red-brown. Each tribe has a particular colour preference and will use no other. By unaccountable instinct the choice yields a rare and striking harmony between their dress and the dignity of the landscape.

With the spread of education, ancestral worship is dying out. All educated and chool-going Africans have accepted Christianity and wear western-style dress. They do not use ochre nor do they participate in tribal dancing or singing. As a result they have lost the art of making beadwork and tribal dress. Western civilisation is weaving new social patterns and a whole new generation has arisen. In the Transkei of rapidly changing outlook, behaviour and fashion, even the typical round huts are being replaced by square, zinc-roofed buildings. Thus the traditional way of life is no longer found throughout the territory but is restricted to small areas untouched by schools and Christianity.

The coastline of the Transkei stretches 450 kilometres, from the Great Kei to the Umtamvuna River. The Drakensberg Mountains form the inland border and run roughly parallel to the coastline at a distance of about 140 kilometres. Rivers form the natural boundaries between the tribes. A map showing the distribution of the tribes appears at the front of the book, but it must be stressed that this is not a uniform or exclusive distribution but merely a general distribution of their whereabouts.

Furthermore, in the naming of the tribes only the stem has been used. This form, although incorrect in Xhosa is commonly accepted in English usage because it obviates the intricacies of the language. In the same way, the term (ama)Xhosa is loosely and collectively applied to the tribal complex, whereas a study of the genealogical table shows that the Xhosa in the Transkei constitute one tribe, this being the Gcaleka. The remaining members of this nation are found beyond the borders of the Transkei in the territory of the Ciskei.

CHAPTER II

GCALEKALAND

*I*n their great migration southwards as the tribes moved along the coast to the Great Kei River, the Xhosa were in the advance guard. Pre-eminent among them was the Gcaleka tribe. They formed the spearhead and occupied a large area, even as far inland as the Drakensberg Mountains. Looked upon as the aristocrats, they were well known for their pride of race, courage and manly bearing. But in 1857 the tribe was involved in a cattle-killing delusion as a result of which they were decimated by famine. It was not, however, until the 9th Frontier War of 1877 that they lost their supremacy. Nevertheless to this day the Gcaleka are regarded as the true Xhosa and are reputed to speak the purest language.

Today Gcalekaland lies between the Great Kei and Bashee rivers and occupies the districts of Kentani and Willowvale. In 1967 I spent several months on the Willowvale coast studying the tribal customs and collecting their beadwork. Despite great strides in education, tribal life was still to be found in abundance. Age grouping, circumcision, initiation into manhood and womanhood, paying of bride price and marriage, all were indissolubly linked with tribal life and gave it meaning, discipline and endeavour. The physique, poise and natural beauty of the people impressed me greatly. In addition, their beadwork appeared more beautiful than that of other tribes. I, therefore, decided that the Gcaleka tribe should be among one of our most important assignments, and that it would be necessary to photograph them during all seasons but particularly during the harvest and seed-planting. For these reasons it was essential that Alice Mertens and I have a permanent base in Gcalekaland.

To this end my husband and I made application to the Transkei Government for permission to purchase a holiday cottage on the wild coast of Gcalekaland. These cottages are hard to come by. Over the years traders and old residents have built a limited number of holiday homes along the coast. Any Transkeian resident is permitted to buy the building from the previous owner, subject to the approval of the Transkeian Government which then issues a certificate of occupation. By good fortune, an old friend offered to sell us her cottage. It was on a delightful and completely unspoilt little bay called Mazeppa. We immediately submitted an application to the magistrate in Kentani and then to the higher officials of government in Umtata. Each time the purpose of the book was explained and our reason for a base camp in Gcalekaland given.

We made our application in December but were informed that the members of this board only met in March. We encountered no difficulties and in March were notified that our application had been accepted and our certificate of occupation granted. It seemed a particularly happy omen that we received our permit two days before Easter and were thus enabled to set off immediately for our first holiday at the cottage.

It is built on the water's edge within sight and sound of the sea. Great white-crested waves sweep across the bay and break in spumes of spray on a rocky island that stretches like a giant crocodile below us. Near us are several white-washed holiday cottages and a hotel.

I used this first holiday for reconnaissance and to get to know the local Africans. Each day at low tide the women from the nearby kraals come down to the shore to collect shellfish, mainly mussels, oysters, venus ears and bait. They sell what they can to the hotel and then go from door to door to the cottages. Whatever is not sold is taken home for their families to eat.

Every day I bought from every woman who came to our door. We had far and away more seafood than either my husband and I or our servants could eat, and as a result our two Siamese cats lived sumptuously and developed extravagant tastes. But if the cats were happy I was even more so. I was making friends with the local women and they were just as beautiful as those I had studied. Furthermore they formed a good cross-section of the community for they included teenagers, young married women, and one or two really old women. Every day I held long conversations with them in Xhosa.

After a few days I showed them my book *Red Blanket Valley*. They exclaimed with pleasure at the pictures of tribal beadwork and dress. I then explained that in June I would return with Alice Mertens and that she was a talented photographer who wanted to take pictures of the Gcaleka beadwork and dress.

I made two very good friends. One was a very beautiful woman called Nomhle (the pretty one) and the other was an old woman called Noyonk'. Both assured me that after the harvest there would be many tribal gatherings and promised that Alice and I would be made welcome. Throughout the Transkei the crops are reaped in June and the harvest is celebrated with tribal functions, particularly initiation ceremonies. It seemed all so easy that I had some misgivings, wondering if they had really accepted me, but both proved loyal friends and Noyonk', particularly, was most helpful.

Further inland I contacted two old trading families, both of whom promised to assist us and introduce us in their areas. Their promises were fulfilled and particular mention must be made of Leon Wood and his wife who gave most generously of their time and hospitality. Before leaving Mazeppa, I checked again with the magistrate in Kentani to make certain that our permits were in order. All was set and I returned to Engcobo for another term's teaching.

In June when the schools closed Alice flew from Cape Town to East London where my husband and I met her. As we drove to Mazeppa Bay we passed through the rugged valley of the Kei River and so into Gcalekaland. The Kei hillsides were bright with red aloes and splashes of pale blue plumbago. Beyond Butterworth we left the national road and followed a dirt road through lovely and unspoilt country. The rivers in their steep and rapid descent to the coast have carved the seaward escarpment into numerous little valleys and gorges so that the hills lie fold upon fold as in the Valley of a Thousand Hills. Being winter the brown of the veld contrasted vividly with the light orange ochre worn by the Gcaleka — a colour choice incredibly in keeping with the undisturbed tranquillity of the land.

The mealie crop had been harvested and the cattle allowed into the lands to graze upon the dried mealies. The herdboys were enjoying a holiday as were their parents, for as we drove between the huts we saw that beer parties were the order of the day.

Beer drinking is one of the most characteristic customs of tribal life. Beer is brewed for all special occasions such as when a beast is sacrificed to propitiate the ancestors, and for all special ceremonies such as initiation, marriage and tribal dances. In addition it is brewed for ordinary social parties called 'Beer-drinks' for beer fulfils a double need, that of food and

4

celebration. After a particularly good harvest beer is brewed daily. It is the accepted rule that every kraal takes its turn in giving a beer-drink and in so doing returns hospitality. No invitations are issued but all are welcome, even passing travellers, for tribal life enjoys a very humane and classless society. Teenagers and young adults do not attend beer-drinks; they have their own parties and dances at which beer is served.

The beer is made from mealies which are ground on a hollowed stone; water is added to the meal and also a small quantity of sprouted corn to hasten fermentation. It is made in great wooden barrels in large quantities. At a beer-drink the men and women gather between the cattlefold and the huts. They sit in a circle on the grass. The hostess fills several cans of beer and these are passed from guest to guest. Each one drinks for as long as he or she has breath and then passes the can on. All smoke pipes and usually a home-grown tobacco and, in a leisurely day of drinking each person consumes a gallon or more of beer. The first time I met Noyonk' I thought her hoarse and raspy voice was the result of too much tobacco and beer. My assumption proved correct. She knew where every beer-drink was in progress and was ever eager to escort us.

Soon our days at Mazeppa set into a steady routine. Early each morning while Alice packed and checked her cameras I packed our lunch basket. Then we drove to the nearest beer-drink. Often we had to wait for proceedings to warm up. I sat and chatted to the people while Alice arranged where she wished to stand with her cameras. We soon discovered that the grass was infested with small red ticks but the discomfort they caused was forgotten in our joy at the wealth and beauty of tribal life.

The Gcaleka are very attractive and gay people. In skin colouring they tend to be lighter than the inland tribes. They also have a more slender build, finer features and, in particular, beautifully shaped eyes. The younger women have a glowing translucent beauty. Their choice of tribal bead colours is entirely appropriate. A bright light turquoise is contrasted with scarlet, navy and white. In the older generation the scarlet is replaced by pink. They do not grow their hair but keep it cut very short. For formal and smart occasions the women wear magnificent turbans made of a dark coloured melton.

For the ordinary beer-drink no one dresses up but when beer is brewed for a special occasion beadwork and smart clothes are worn. The women wear a wide, flared skirt made of a coarse white cloth that is braided from hip to hem, and a small white apron or bib covers the breasts. Their dress is very elegant and is especially attractive during the dances when their skirts spin. The men wear white woollen blankets. Sometimes they fold them like a skirt but usually they wear them like a toga and with the same majesty and dignity.

One day Noyonk' told us that a certain kraal had brewed beer for a special occasion. She said she would meet us there because it would take her time to dress. The guests gathered slowly in two's and three's. The men and women were a resplendent sight. In keeping with the dignity of her age, Noyonk' wore a large cart-wheel turban and over her right arm she carried a most decorative goatskin bag. It measured over a metre and was made of an entire goat skin — the pelt having been removed from the carcass intact. After drying and curing, the skin had been turned inside out with the hair on the inside. The leather had been decorated with beads. Both men and women carry these highly ornamental bags and we saw them in no other tribe. In addition to their lovely necklaces and headbands, most adults of standing wear a simple but very beautiful necklace of shells. Among the Gcalekas this necklace holds pride of place, and its simplicity and beauty is in keeping with the nobility of the tribe.

Most of the beer-drinks had been festive and jolly parties but this one got off to a flying start. The beer cans had barely circulated when a well-dressed but portly middle-aged man started to dance and called upon a younger woman to join him. In no time the women had formed a circle, swaying to the rhythm of their song, beating time with their hands and feet. Drawn into the music, one woman at a time would leave the circle and join the dancers in the centre. A half-smile on her face, arms raised like a Geisha she performed all the ritual gestures. But one man stole the show. He was not well dressed. One of the women whispered to me that he had encountered a little domestic trouble and that his wife had locked away his party clothes and refused to hand over the key. But this in no way detracted from the gay Lothario's enjoyment. He was the highlight of the party — dancing, burlesqueing, clowning and pandering to his audience — he had us all in fits of laughter. Alice laughed so much she had to stop photographing.

That afternoon we returned to the cottage, windburnt, tick-bitten but happy. Each night Alice developed the black and white films. Then when they were dry we held them against the light to scrutinise and assess them. Our hearts beat fast. We could see it all: the beauty, the pulsating rhythm and the exuberant vitality. My optimism and belief in the Gcaleka had been justified.

In the days that followed we attended teenage dances, dances for young adults, initiation ceremonies and witchdoctor rituals. All these will be described in the introduction to each group of photographs.

CHAPTER III

TEMBULAND

*I*n July we left the sea cottage and journeyed to Tembuland to the village of Engcobo where I was born and have spent the greater part of my life. Greater Tembuland lies in the uplands of the western Transkei and comprises two tribes: the Tembu and the Emigrant Tembu. Their territory stretches from the upper reaches of the Great Kei River, known as the White Kei, to the Umtata River.

The Emigrant Tembu live beyond the White Kei River in the lee of the Stormberg Mountains where they occupy the districts of Cala and Cofimvaba. Emigrant Tembuland received its name in 1865 when Governor Philip Wodehouse settled a section of the Tembu who, in the disturbances of the 1820's * had fled to what is now known as the division of Queenstown. When this section was annexed to the Cape Colony they agreed to an exchange of land and returned. They were therefore known as Emigrant Tembu. The Paramount Chief of the Emigrant Tembu is the Honourable Kaizer Daliwonga Matanzima who is also the present Prime Minister of the Transkei.

The Tembu tribe occupy the districts of Engcobo, Umtata and Mqanduli. They give allegiance to Sabata Dalindyebo. The Tembu and Emigrant Tembu are closely related — their chiefs, Sabata and Kaizer, are cousins, being the great-grandsons of Paramount Chief Umtirara. Both are his heirs. The Dalindyebos are descended from the royal house, that is from the first wife, and the Matanzimas from the right-hand house or second wife. Tribal lore binds the tribes, for certain customs pertaining to the royal house of the Tembu must according to tradition, be performed by the heir to the right-hand house, that is by the chief of the Emigrant Tembu and vice versa. Ancestral faith evokes an astonishing response and this force of tradition adds strength and affection to the bonds of kinship and co-operation. Physically the tribes are similar and they share the same customs, beadwork and dress.

In the early days when the Tembu tribe was driven westward by the pressure of the Zulu armies, it gave sanctuary to several sub-tribes who had fled at the approach of the renowned Zulus. These sub-tribes became vassals to the Tembu but being of alien blood they lacked the religious bond of a common ancestor and until they were absorbed they were a weakening influence. The strength of the Tembu tribe dates from the 9th Frontier War of 1877. In this war the Gcaleka tribe declared war upon the Fingos. The Fingos were British subjects and so the Government of the Cape Colony championed them. During the

---

* They had fled from the rest of their tribe because of attacks upon them by the dreaded Mfecane who were themselves fugitives from Shaka's reign of terror.

previous year, the Tembu Chief Ngangelizwe had also become a British subject and promised his tribe's allegiance to the British crown. It was an allegiance of honour which was readily understood and soon to be proved. When called upon to join the struggle, the Tembu levies in their thousands went to the assistance of the Fingos, and the Gcalekas were defeated and their supreme authority broken.

Today Sabata Dalindyebo is the supreme chief and hereditary ruler of more than 500 000 Tembus. His presence is always hailed by the salute of *Ah Jonguhlanga* (shepherd of the people). The Tembu associate themselves easily and strongly with loyalty and this characteristic more than any other binds them.

They have the same tribal customs as the Gcalekas. They practise circumcision, initiation into manhood and womanhood, payment of bride price and polygamy but they differ in personality and physique. They are heavier in build and features, and darker in colour. They have strong faces full of expression, patience and power. One senses a strength and stability of character. They are not as volatile as the Gcalekas but nevertheless they are a vivacious and happy people.

Tembuland is very beautiful. It is undulating country. Softly rounded hills and wooded valleys lead through a rolling staircase of hills to the high forest-clad slopes, to the waterfalls and the long line of precipices that run northwards to the Drakensberg Mountain. This dark blue mountain rises in a clear outline. Its face, uncompromising, precipitous and inaccessible, dominates the landscape.

The Tembu cultivate lands of maize, beans and pumpkins. Many own considerable herds of cattle, sheep and goats. As farmers they appear more prosperous than the Gcalekas. Tembuland is well grassed and the mountain grazing is good. The cattle look sleek and there are not so many ticks.

It was far easier to obtain photographs in Tembuland for I was in home territory and had the support of my African friends. Some like Mrs Ndosi Poswayo's family had been close family friends for four generations and so it was that we constantly turned to her for assistance. In the foothills and valleys of the Drakensberg, tribal life exists as it has for centuries. We had only to travel up 'Red Blanket Valley', call on one or two of her friends and watch their daily life in the kraals to become aware of the ancient rhythm of Africa: the nursing mother painting her face white before setting out or decorating her baby's face or dressing her two-year-old in beads. Wherever one looks one sees the picturesque women carrying headloads of firewood, or women carrying buckets of water or beer barrels or baskets filled with pumpkins and green mealie cobs. They walk beautifully, their head-loads perfectly balanced. Sometimes a bangled arm reaches up to steady a bucket or to pacify the little black baby that rides naked on its mother's back. Each time one is struck afresh by the graceful carriage, the quick smiles, the faces glowing with good humour and the warm and cordial greetings. In place of the orange-red ochre of the Gcalekas the Tembus use a deeper, richer red.

It is simple to tell the difference between a married woman and a young unmarried girl. The married woman wears the long swaying ankle-length skirt, braided at the hem. A straight, narrow bib or apron is tied above the breasts and hangs to well below the knees where it touches the first line of braid. Across her shoulders she folds a red-ochred shawl or uses it to strap her baby to her back. The unmarried girl wears a short skirt. The young teenager wears a short wrap-around skirt to above her knees. Her elder sister wears a flared skirt, mid-calf in length. Neither covers the top of the torso but exposes the breasts. Traditional or tribal dress predominates among the women and girls but the men usually wear western dress and carry a blanket. The tribal dress of the men is to be seen at the weekends and on special occasions when they wear their traditional white skirts and shawls. On these occasions the women favour skirts made from soft oxhide or beaten sheep pelts. In either case the hairless side is worn on the outside.

Both sexes decorate their limbs with brass leggings, armbands and wristlets. These are hand-made from tightly spiralled brass wire. In addition all wear small hoop ear-rings of chrome and a small quantity of beadwork. For ceremonial occasions they wear full tribal bead-dress consisting of many necklaces, head bands, arm bands, leg bands, body harnesses and girdles or belts. Tembu head colours are more sombre and dignified than the Gcaleka. A darker duller blue replaces the bright turquoise of the Gcaleka and red is used sparingly and only as a contrasting colour to navy and white. In all tribal celebrations there is the age-old fascination expressed in beadwork, song and dance. They are the symbols of sound and beauty that communicate a special meaning and give an extra dimension to the life of the tribe.

The weekends are usually reserved for beer-drinks and tribal dances. These functions are strictly constituted in age groups. Each dance has its place in the life of the tribe and it is important that each age group conforms and keeps this balance. There are dances for teenagers, for young adults and for the middle-aged and more mature. My friends were kind enough to allow us to attend these dances, and so Alice was able to photograph teenagers in charming dress, young adults in princely bead apparel and the older men who hold the greatest tribal prestige and are therefore the most impressive in the dignity and beauty of their tribal dress. We were fortunate to be the guests in Emigrant Tembuland at a dance to celebrate a girl's initiation into womanhood. This is danced and attended entirely by women. The grace and elegance of the women and the exquisite styles of their dress and beadwork are shown in the photographs.

There are many witchdoctors in Tembuland, particularly in the mountainous regions where their impact appears to be stronger than in Gcalekaland. This may be due to the close proximity of the great mountains and forests, for the tribal African has a strange idea about medicine. He believes that somewhere on the mountains or in the forests plants are to be found that will cure every illness. He believes that a witchdoctor who is true to his calling will be led to these plants by his animal medium and that thereafter the therapeutic power of the plants is his secret.

It must also be borne in mind that until the middle of the last century Bushmen clans were to be found living in the foothills of the Drakensberg. In the valleys their caves and rock paintings are still to be seen. Although the Bushmen had no witchdoctors as such, they had rain doctors. In dry seasons the Tembu tribe employed these Bushman rain doctors to bring rain for them. It may be coincidence but the sacred forest of the witchdoctors lies close to where the last of the Bushmen clan lived. Be that as it may, the witchdoctors have an intuitive understanding of African psychology and many are the stories of the efficacy of their tribal remedies. An old trader once told me that he had received treatment from a witchdoctor who immunised against snake-bite by making an incision and applying a powder. The same witchdoctor could heal fractured bones. An ox with a badly broken leg was treated and within two months the fracture had knitted so well that he was back in the plough.

I know all the witchdoctors in 'Red Blanket Valley' and am on particularly friendly terms with several of the witchdoctresses. Through one of them I learned that there was to be a very great gathering of witchdoctors and I made arrangements for Alice to attend. All told there were sixteen witchdoctors and their acolytes but although the witchdoctor-in-chief permitted photographs to be taken of their initial parade he would not allow any other photographs to be taken. He said that the ceremony was of a private nature and that only members of the priesthood could attend. Long afterwards I ascertained that they had gathered to honour the spirits of a deceased witchdoctor.

CHAPTER IV

PONDOLAND

*O*ur next assignment was Pondoland. It is not only the most beautiful part of the Transkei but it is also steeped in history and romance. At some period in the long distant past, a huge earth movement or quake lifted up Pondoland, splitting its mountains and leaving steep-sided cliffs with sheer rock faces. Between the rifts in the mountains one looks down into the enormous depths of great V-shaped valleys where two or more rivers converge. At certain places along the coast the rocks fall sheer to the sea and, depending on how rough the sea is, when the waves dash against the wall they send their spray hundreds of metres into the air. At one spot called Waterfall Bluff, a waterfall drops over the face of a precipice into the sea. Inland there are many lovely waterfalls — the Tsitsa, Fraser, Picnic, Ntentule and Magwa, the last named being higher than the Victoria Falls. There is so much beauty that it is breathtaking.

It is easy to understand that the first Africans to see the Tina River exclaimed in surprise and joy *Thina-Wethu* (Oh bless us). Thus the name Tina was given. Likewise the Umzimvubu, the largest and most beautiful river in the Transkei was named "The home of the Hippo". There are no more hippos, but the occasional python and mamba are to be seen. The climate is tropical and great tree ferns fill the gorges, and dense forest grows to the water's edge. The rainfall is the highest in the Republic and the soil is rich and black. Pawpaws, bananas, guavas and other tropical fruits flourish.

The richness and beauty of the territory is matched by its history. One hundred years before Jan van Riebeeck landed at the Cape, Portuguese sailing vessels had been wrecked on the Pondoland coast and survivors had lived to tell their tale. Then in 1552, the Portuguese galleon *Saoa* was wrecked. At that time the territory was occupied by the Xhosa: the Pondo tribe arrived a century later. The survivors from this wreck were kindly received, as were those from the many wrecks that followed — Portuguese, Dutch and English. Some survivors lived on among the Africans, taking African husbands or wives and traces of this ancestry are still to be seen in their progeny. Others attempted to return overland via Mozambique or the Cape. Few survived the terrible ordeal but their stories brought explorers, adventurers, remittance men, gunrunners, fugitives from the law; even the first Sinn Feiners sought their sanctuary or Shangri-la in Pondoland. These were colourful characters.

In the last century Eastern Pondoland was a turbulent territory. The Xhosa had moved to the land beyond the Umtata River and the Pondo tribe was living on the banks of the Umzimvubu. But they were constantly under pressure from the Zulus and from

10

fragmented tribes and clans fleeing from the armies of Shaka. Dread of this invading host and the terror inspired by the marauders shaped the life of the Pondo tribe.

Today Pondoland lies between the Umtata and Umtamvuna rivers, and is divided by the Umzimvubu into Western and Eastern Pondoland. Paramount Victor Poto rules Western Pondoland and has his great place at Libode, while Botha Sigcau, whose great place is at Lusikisiki, is the Paramount Chief of Eastern Pondoland.

In preparation for our Pondoland assignment I had been in correspondence with a close friend of my father's, a Mr Frank Daniel of Port St Johns, an octogenarian who all his life had traded in Pondoland, and is a recognised authority and linguist. He had kindly offered to accompany us on our Pondoland venture. Therefore, in September, I spent a weekend in Port St Johns to finalise arrangements. From the outset he warned that tribal dress and beadwork were rapidly disappearing from Pondoland. Nevertheless, drawing on his intimate knowledge, he drew up an itinerary pinpointing the areas most suitable for our work. Both he and his wife, Maud, my father's cousin, were a constant source of strength and information.

At the beginning of December, Alice arrived from Stellenbosch. The weather was perfect: there were a few white clouds but a beautiful blue sky and glorious views of mountains, valleys and grassy plains.

We crossed the Umtata River into Western Pondoland and in a very short time were at Libode. But we did not stop, for we had arranged to meet Frank some twenty-five kilometres away at the foot of the Mlengane Pass. We were making good time and soon, around a bend across a beautiful valley, rose the towering dome of the Mlengane Mountain. It is an unusual sight — a massive rock that is shaped like a huge grey fortress. Its sides are precipitous but the flat top is covered with green grass. We stopped for Alice to take photographs. The road traverses the very foot of the rock and later we stopped again. The rock loomed right over us. As a child I had always feared that one of the long overhanging precipices that appear to cling precariously, would come hurtling down but they are still firmly fixed in position.

We were a little late for our appointment. When we got out to greet Maud and Frank it was fiercely hot and we wasted no time. Frank led us off the main road and up the magnificent Mjolo Pass. Higher up it was cooler and we stopped to look down the long deep gorge of the Umgazi River. It was an entrancing sight and while we waited we saw our first blue-blanketed Pondos. The Pondo tribe use blue instead of red ochre.

Seventy years ago when the great chief, Marhelane, of Eastern Pondoland died, his people, as a sign of mourning, gave up the use of red ochre and wore white which is the traditional colour of mourning. However, it was difficult to keep the blankets and tribal dress a good shining white and one day a woman, in an attempt to whiten her husband's blanket used a packet of blue. She used too much and the blanket came out a very pretty duck-egg blue. The colour was an immediate success. The Pondos loved this particular shade of blue and forthwith started to *blue* their blankets and tribal dress. Their old maroon red ochre was a thing of the past and was never used again. In changing they made a charming choice. The blue looks cool and is more in keeping with the dark greens of the tropical landscape than the deep maroon red. Nevertheless for many years the people of Western Pondoland continued to use this ochre but later many of them changed to the blue colour. The colour of their beadwork matches the blue of their blanket, for the Pondos use pale turquoise beads contrasted with white, black and orange.

The Pondo tribe does not practise circumcision and there is no initiation into manhood or womanhood. Many other traditions have lapsed and there is a general laxity. Bride price, as such, is seldom paid in full. Girls marry or are carried off at the early age of thirteen or fourteen years. The old tribal dance steps have been replaced by modern jive and Zulu dances are creeping in. There is nothing like the rigid age grouping and strongly constituted tribal life of the Tembu and Gcaleka.

In physical characteristics too, they are markedly different. Although smaller in build their features and faces are slightly wider and carry scarification marks. The women grow their hair. They start in early teenage and women wear it shoulderlength plaited in thin threads. Others take spun thread or yarn which they plait into their hair where it hangs in a long mane down the back. All married women pull a twist or thin fringe to the front. It is rolled in soft wire and the resulting curl rests on or above the nose. Married women also wear the beautifully beaded wedding or head ring. This is usually held in position on the head by means of a long snuff spoon. The latter has a long handle and is delicately fashioned from horn. All Pondos — men, women and teenagers, are inveterate takers of snuff. It is a habit-forming practice. At the tender age of ten years the young girls are taught to prepare the snuff. It is made from aloe and tobacco leaves finely ground and blended to individual taste.

As we travelled to Majola we saw the authentic execution rock which the tribe used until the end of the last century. The Mlengane rock is sometimes mistakenly called execution rock but this is a misnomer. At the rock on the Majola Pass the tribe executed sorcerers, murderers, cattle thieves and unfaithful wives. The witchdoctors supposedly 'smelt out' these evil-doers. When some one was about to be smelt out an interesting code warning was employed. A friend whispered the word *inyanda*. In Xhosa this means a head-load of wood. In the early days and as late as the last century the Umzimvubu was a wide, fast-flowing river up which sailing vessels and small steamers travelled. Today it has silted up but then it was so deep that it could only be forded at isolated drifts. Any other crossing from Eastern Pondoland into Western Pondoland necessitated floating across the river and the Africans employed an ingenious device. A headload of wood was used as a float. A man or woman clung to the wood which floated and was carried by the current to the opposite bank. In this manner victims about to be smelt out, sought the safety and refuge of Western Pondoland for it was a peaceful and stable community.

As we journeyed we noticed that the huts and homesteads were built on the high ridges and that the arable lands lay in the valleys. This is a carry-over from the days of the tribal wars. During the last century there was constant warfare waged by the Pondos against the Bhaca and Xesibe tribes and other clans who were being pressed into their territory by the Zulus. On the borders of Pondoland there were raids and counter-raids with frequent loss of life. In reprisal the Bhacas and Xesibes invaded Pondoland, looting kraals and stealing women and cattle. Therefore the Pondos built their kraals on the ridges of the hills, for these positions afforded the highest vantage. They could look out and shout a warning from one hill to the other, that the enemy was approaching. The raiders never murdered the women and children but carried them off. Afterwards if they were recovered their families identified them by their facial scarifications. Today the need for scarification has fallen away but the custom is continued as a form of facial decoration.

At Majola which is very beautiful the scenery is much like the highlands of Kenya. Similar too, in climate for no frost is experienced. Therefore the Xhosa Government has established a large experimental station where tea, coffee and cotton are most successfully grown. Later on we saw larger areas of this cultivation at Lusikisiki, the most southerly tea plantations in the world. From Majola we followed the Umzimvubu as it winds its glorious way through precipitous cliffs and mountains. Twenty kilometres from the river mouth we looked across the great height of the valley to Ntili. The old wagon tracks still shone on the hills and the view from the top is truly panoramic. The wagon tracks are all that remain of the first overland route from Durban to Cape Town. This was the route used by the first pioneers: survivors of the earliest shipwrecks, traders, missionaries, military and magistrates. Their names are enshrined in the history of Pondoland and South Africa. Here too, Dick King rode in his famous ride from Durban to Grahamstown.

We looked down at the still broad river, at the drift he forded, and our eyes followed the steep ascent up which he toiled. In this lonely and lovely sweep of country with its extraordinary beauty, one is stirred not only by the beauty but also by the memory of the early pioneers. At its mouth the Umzimvubu runs through a huge cleft in the mountain and then into the sea. It is guarded on each side by great buttresses of sheer rock known as the 'Gates'. On one of the krantzes of the Eastern Gate stands silhouetted against the sky, a full-length rock statue of a man in cowl and hood. He looks benevolently towards the sea. Legend tells that during the seventeenth century Portuguese sailors saw this figure and believing it to be St John, the Apostle, gave the name Port St Johns. It is well named for the gates open on a dazzling panorama — an exquisite meeting of sky, sea and earth.

From Port St Johns we visited trading stations in Eastern Pondoland but our best day was when we drove with Frank on a rough dirt road to a tiny trading station in the Lusikisiki district. It was an isolated spot, in a fold of the hills and he held high hopes of our seeing tribal dress and beadwork. But on our arrival we were most disappointed to find very few customers and no tribal dress. The customers said that most people were attending a beer-drink on the hill. Fortunately Frank was well known to the people and on friendly terms with them, and so we were taken to the kraal on the hill.

A Pondo beer-drink is quite different from that of any other tribe which we attended. The first difference is that the beer is drunk from a beer basket. The basket is beautifully woven from fine grass. The weave is so close and even that the surface is completely sealed and watertight. The basket is a convenient size to hold and carries about four litres.

The next difference we noted is that each man sits upon a beer stool. The Pondo men make these small, low stools from the soft wood of the Cabbage Tree (*Cussonia spicata*). When the stool is completed it is decorated by burning a geometrical design into the wood with a hot wire. The stool is extremely light and it is usually carried to the beer-drink by the man's mistress.

At this beer-drink, blue blankets, cascades of fringed necklaces, chains of turquoise and white beads, head rings, snuff spoons, long plaited hair — all were in evidence. We had a wonderful morning. The Transkeians have coined a phrase 'Pondoland Fever'. It is used to describe a state in which the individual is too contented and happy to undertake any form of serious employment. In the magic of that morning I realised that the cause of Pondoland Fever is that those who suffer from it have come to know that prosperity is not happiness. In Pondoland happiness is drinking beer, seeing and feeling the sunlight and watching the clouds go by.

CHAPTER V

BOMVANALAND

*T*he next few days we spent with friends in Lusikisiki but unfortunately we encountered three days of rain. In between breaks in the weather we parked the car on the roadside and waited for Christmas shoppers to pass while Alice used a telephoto lens. On another occasion we were richly rewarded when we sat and waited at the bus stop in the village. There we saw several Pondo women in tribal dress but one particular couple held our attention. A man and his young wife were seated near a gate, his luggage beside them. The woman looked about thirteen or fourteen years old and although she was drooping with fatigue she was exquisite. Her features, expressions and gestures held us enthralled. At one stage she peeled and handed her husband an orange and her entire movement was a study in elegance and natural grace.

When the weather cleared we were taken by our host on a tour of scenic splendour. We visited Horse-Shoe Bend at Tabankulu, saw wonderful views of the Umzimvubu valley, the Magwa and Fraser falls and the magnificent coastline. Wherever we glimpsed traditional tribal life we paused and were never disappointed. Once it was the familiar sight of two young teenagers stamping mealies on a wooden block. Another time at a beer-drink, I heard in the distance the faint throb of a witchdoctor's drum and on enquiring was told that the witchdoctors were gathering to dance but the venue was several kilometres distant.

From Lusikisiki we returned via Port St Johns to Umtata and proceeded to visit the Bomvana tribe. Bomvanaland lies contiguous to Western Pondoland. Although the Bomvanas and Pondos originated from the same branch, the Bomvanas have identified themselves strongly with the Tembu tribe. The reason being that in 1885 when Emigrant Tembuland and Tembuland were incorporated into the Cape Colony, Bomvanaland was included to form part of a United Tembuland. Nevertheless the Bomvanas have remained a distinct tribe. Although similar in tribal dress to the Tembu, their ochre is a brighter orange and the colours of their beadwork and design are also different.

The tribe occupies the coastal area between the Bashee and Umtata rivers. Thus it includes the whole of the Elliotdale district and the lower part of the Mqanduli district. Geographically, Bomvanaland and Pondoland are similar. They share the same tropical climate and their coastline shows the same signs that at some era there was a great upheaval and rejuvenation of the earth's crust.

From Umtata we travelled to Mqanduli and then on towards the wild coast. Our first stop was at a well-known trading station that overlooks the Umtata River. The young trader, a third generation Transkeian, had been most helpful. Not only had he offered to

14

accommodate us in his cottage at Coffee Bay but he had also spoken to the local chief who had invited us to visit his great place and to meet Bomvanas in tribal dress. These invitations we accepted with alacrity.

Yet surprisingly and significantly our most rewarding pictures were taken at the trading store. It wanted five days to Christmas and then the trader was going away on holiday and he would not return until mid-January, and as a result there were literally hundreds of customers. From early morning until late afternoon they stood in a long queue. The blue blankets of the Pondos who had crossed the Umtata River mingled with the orange ochre of the Bomvanas. As the queue moved slowly forward we had ample time to compare their tribal dress.

The trading station is ideally situated on a knoll above the Umtata River and for us it proved a fairy knoll. It overlooked the blue depths of the great valley, with its riot of smaller valleys and gorges folded one upon the other. The customers who had completed their shopping sat in the shade of a magnificent wild fig tree. Men sat smoking, women gossiped happily while others fed their babies. A good day's enjoyment is always to be had chatting and gossiping at the trading store. It makes a fine rendezvous, especially for the teenagers.

From our position a short distance away we looked upon the long queue waiting to buy, and then out across the valley to the steep foot-paths that zigzagged their way up the hills bringing more customers. From afar we would see the upright graceful figures, effortlessly ascending the steepest paths. They would disappear from sight and reappear as they breasted our knoll and Alice's camera would start clicking. We had a glorious time.

Beyond the tree, ox-drawn sleighs were being loaded with bags of mealies. Periodically a man would call an instruction to a small boy who was waiting to lead the oxen. Teenage girls and women were being assisted to raise large sacks of meal on to their heads. This accomplished they wasted no time but set off walking at an incredibly fast pace.

For those in the queue there was no shelter, but they did not seem to mind the heat. One or two placed shopping bags on their heads as hats. Another girl played a Xhosa harp. This is made from a curve of wood joined by a single brass strand. While the player holds the bow in her mouth, she blows the tune and twangs the wire with a grass stem, thus producing flute-like tunes. In the queue I noticed three girls wearing a very deep maroon, almost brown, ochre — the richness of which would have graced an old master's palette. I approached them but they were very shy and turned their faces away. Eventually I ascertained that they were Pondos and that this particular shade of ochre is still used. The depth of colour is obtained by mixing the ochre with oil. The whole garment is smeared with vaseline or fat and the ochre sprinkled on then rubbed in. The girls were sisters. They had good features and unusually beautiful hands.

In comparison with the Pondo tribe, tribal life is strong. The Bomvanas practise circumcision and all the ceremonies of initiation into manhood and womanhood. Thus their society is firmly constituted in age groups. Bride price is paid in full and usually eight to ten head of cattle are required. Although there is some inter-marriage between the two tribes the Bomvanas deplore the laxity of the Pondos and consider themselves to be far superior. They say that the Pondo men are 'mere boys' because they have not been circumcised and that this accounts for their lack of responsibility. Be that as it may, the Bomvana teenagers have not been above copying the 'duck-egg blue' of the Pondo. We saw a Bomvana girl on her way to a teenage dance. She was wearing a delightful short 'blued' skirt in conjunction with her orange-ochred shawl. On being questioned she replied that it was a popular combination. Other unique features of the Bomvana teenage dress are the beaded leggings which the girls wear just below the knee. These comprise rows of large pearl-like coloured beads decorated with smaller beaded tags.

From the trading store we travelled to Coffee Bay, a holiday resort on the coast. It derives its name from a ship that was wrecked in the last century. She was carrying a cargo of raw chocolate, rum and coffee beans. Casks of coffee beans littered the shore and so the name Coffee Bay was given. The scenery is inspiring — white stretches of beach backed by forest-clad hills and cliffs.

Like Pondoland, the coast of Bomvanaland is endowed with the glamour of the past. Here, too, from the sixteenth century onwards, first Portuguese, then Dutch and later English vessels returning richly laden from the Far East, drifted out of the Agulhas current, and the force of the west winds drove them on to the rocks.

The first record of a shipwreck at the Umtata river-mouth is given as 1554; a little later there was another at Hole in the Wall, then one at the Xora river-mouth. These were followed by many more. It is of particular interest that in almost every wreck, certain of the survivors settled among the Africans. As a result there are in Bomvanaland several well-known, light-complexioned clans who trace their ancestry to the survivors from these wrecks. The most famous survivor was a seven-year-old girl who called herself 'Bessie'. Later she married a chief and exerted great influence. Thus Bomvanaland is full of romance and nowhere is one more aware of this than at Hole in the Wall.

This lies several kilometres south of Coffee Bay. There is no hotel or store only a row of holiday cottages dotted along the shore. A cousin of mine had lent me his beautiful cottage and so we spent some days at this glorious spot. At the mouth of the river lies a massive mountain barrier through which the pounding surf and the river have worn a large tunnel. As the waves surge through the tunnel they break against the inner wall creating a beautiful spray. On the eastern side of this wall is a great hill known as 'Whale's Back' — its shape indicating the name. Next to this is a narrow chasm hundreds of metres deep. It is flanked by sheer rock faces which tower overhead. As the waves smash through this narrow chasm they break with untrammelled force against giant boulders and great fragments of rock. It is an awe-inspiring sight. One looks at the sea, then up through the high black rocks to a shaft of light, and one is reminded of first life on earth and of early man.

In this spectacular setting one senses an Africa still primitive and steeped in mystical superstition. The mythology and folk-lore of the Xhosa are to a large extent centred around rivers, particularly deep pools near the sea or river-mouths. These are believed to be specially favoured by the spirits of their dead chiefs who exercise enormous influence over every member of the tribe. This spiritual fantasy still holds sway in Bomvanaland where sacred cattle called *bolowane* are used as propitiatory sacrifices. These cattle are kept at the Great Place or royal kraal of Chief Ngubezulu in the district of Elliotdale. They belong to the royal family and only its members may drink the milk from the cows.

Should a member of the royal family fall ill, the herd is driven to a special deep pool on the Kukapi stream. The first animal to drink is sacrificed and the meat placed around the pool. If the propitiation is favourably received a piece of meat will be drawn into the pool and the patient will recover. If the meat is left untouched the patient will die. Recently a beast was sacrificed to bring rain and it did, in fact, rain. When an animal is sacrificed to bring rain, the women may not partake of the meat. Only the men are permitted to eat it, but thereafter they must immediately go to the river and wash.

CHAPTER VI

THE MPONDOMISE, BHACA AND XESIBE TRIBES

*T*he day before Christmas we left Bomvanaland and returned to Mazeppa Bay, to our cottage on the ocean front. This was to enable Alice to photograph the Gcalekas in the summer and also I had arranged a family party for our first Christmas and New Year at the cottage. We were a large party: Alice, my brother, his wife and two daughters, my sister, my husband and I. Our cottage, like every other cottage, was full to overflowing. Although it was a working holiday it was a pleasant respite. Early each morning we swam in the warm water of the Indian Ocean and fleetingly basked in the sun at our private cove. At night there was the release of the evening walk along the beach, the talks with my family whom I had not seen for a year and the resumption of old friendships. The faithful Noyonk' had been expecting us and accompanied us on many excursions, and again we were not disappointed, for the photographic material was magnificent.

After the New Year we returned to Engcobo to prepare for our visit to the Mpondomise. Our plans had been well laid and our itinerary drawn but in the end Alice had to set off alone, for I was obliged to move house but I joined her two days later in Qumbu.

The Mpondomise comprise 50 000 persons who inhabit the upland corridor between the Drakensberg and the broken coastal strip of Western Pondoland. They are settled in the districts of Qumbu and Tsolo. Although the Mpondomise are genealogically closely linked with the Pondo, they exhibit an interesting blend of Tembu and Mpondo elements owing no doubt to their geographical position between these two powerful tribes.

We had planned to commence our tour of the Mpondomise in the Qumbu district and therefore it was most fortunate that I could contact my friend who was secretary of the Nessie Knight hospital at Sulenkama, and ask her to receive Alice and introduce her to the Mpondomise. Sulenkama is situated 28 kilometres from Qumbu. It lies in a beautiful valley and from the hill above the hospital one looks on to the Drakensberg Mountains which border Lesotho. Throughout the Transkei there are many mission stations and mission hospitals under various denominations. Each has an interesting history but that of Sulenkama is unique. Eighty years ago after the murder of the magistrate by the Mpondomise, the Church of Scotland founded a mission in the area. In 1925 a young doctor, Bert Paterson of Glasgow, went out to Sulenkama to establish a Church of Scotland Medical Mission. Because the only accommodation available was a mud hut he was forced to leave Nessie, his bride of a few months, in Scotland. Soon her husband wrote desperate letters saying he needed a dispensary and a hospital but that there was no money. Nessie Knight Paterson immediately formed a group of young friends from her church into a dramatic club and proceeded to produce two of Sir James Barrie's plays. Glasgow newspapers picked up the story and in a matter of months Nessie joined her husband at Sulenkama taking with her the money needed for the dispensary and hospital. Today the Nessie Knight Hospital has grown from the original mud hut to its present size of 180 beds.

The story has always fascinated me and when my husband and I visited this remarkable mission station we were charmed and delighted not only by the warmth of the welcome accorded to us but by the beauty and the romance. Nessie Knight Paterson is still alive, a widow living in Scotland, but her Gaelic magic and her ability to organise, live on at Sulenkama. When the secretary, Amy Wishart, received my letter asking for her help, she called upon the local chief and explained the purpose of our book. He raised the matter at a meeting of his headmen and as a result a day of tribal dancing in full dress was arranged. It was a great day. Alice supplied the beer and from all accounts it was a fantastic display. Unfortunately I missed it but the next day when I met Alice and Amy they could talk of nothing else. In one hour they had witnessed every age group perform their tribal dances in traditional dress.

The fact that the Mpondomise are of Pondo stock shows in the broadness of their face, the slight coarseness of their features and the heavier, squatter figures. Furthermore they favour the Pondo colour of duck-egg blue and their beadwork is remarkably like Pondo beadwork of a generation ago. I saw turquoise-blue necklaces, beaded ear-rings and beaded hat pins similar to those collected in Pondoland thirty years ago and yet today the Pondos have ceased to make this work. But there the likeness ceases and in other respects the Mpondomise appear to follow the Tembu pattern. They wear their hair cut short and bear no facial scarification marks, and their dress and some of their dances are in Tembu style.

The tribe practises circumcision and performs the corresponding ceremonies of initiation into manhood and womanhood, and thereafter boldly shoulders adult maturity. All tribal functions and dances are arranged in age groups. It is a transcending scale which creates a healthy tribal life. Age grouping strengthens the traditional ties — those priceless and indispensable links with the past. Throughout life each individual identifies with his age group and develops a sense of pride, of dignity and personal worth. He has his place in the ultimate scheme and knows exactly where he stands. It does away with hostility, misunderstanding and social camouflage. It follows that among the Mpondomise payment of bride price is traditional. Where there is a scarcity of cattle up to R200 in money is paid.

In their daily life around the kraals the women of the Mpondomise wear the red-ochred, braided skirts and turbans typical of the Tembu but to parties and dances they wear 'blued' skirts and shawls and establish their individuality in gorgeous head-dresses draped and shaped like a peacock's tail. These are made of two or more turbans decorated with rows of ornamental stitching and folded into a fan of points that are held in place by a galaxy of glittering hat pins. For parties the men like to wear blue blankets attractively edged or bordered with decorative stripes.

From Qumbu we travelled to Mount Frere in which district the Bhaca tribe predominates. Unfortunately their tribal life has all but disappeared. In isolated mountain areas a little is to be found. High in the mountains, a young African trader and his wife introduced us to the only tribal people that we met. These were teenage girls who wore short pleated tunics over beaded skirts, and young men who had returned from the mines and wore elegant wide-legged trousers, bell-bottomed and tied at the ankle for all like Turkish brigands. When they walked their pantaloons billowed out. One of the men played a flute and the girls danced for us. They moved in a straight line forwards then backwards, kicking their legs high. It was a modification of the *indlamu* danced by the Pondos. Like the Pondos the Bhacas do not practise circumcision and there is no differentiation between manhood and boyhood. There is no age grouping; unmarried youths and married men dance with teenage girls. Their famous dance of the first fruits, which was celebrated each year at the Chief's kraal is no longer performed.

Yet strangely enough despite the loss of tribal life in dance and dress, facial scarification is still practised. In this mountainous area, from the age of six months or as soon as a child can sit the grandmother scarifies its face. She makes three incisions on the chin, four on each cheek and seven on the forehead. Then she applies ochre to stop the bleeding. On healing the scars appear as lines on the face. From the age of ten months a small boy wears a little skirt made of two separate pieces of leather — one for the front and one for the back. Called an *ibeshu* the skirt is an exact replica of that worn by the Zulus. As a result of the wars and disturbances attendant upon Shaka's reign, the Bhacas fled from Natal; but after peace and security were restored, many migrated northwards again. Thus a branch of the Bhaca tribe lives in the district of Umzimkulu and many others are to be found in Natal. There is a natural affiliation both in language and custom with the Natal group. We were disappointed not to visit Umzimkulu but there followed two days of rain and mist which blotted out the sky.

We moved on to Mount Ayliff to the Xesibe tribe. The latter had also fled Natal in Shaka's reign. Originally they had occupied land far eastward but they had been steadily forced back by the Pondos whose evil treatment extended over many years. Eventually the Xesibes had settled in the rugged country around Mount Ayliff where, although a small tribe, they were able to defend themselves against the much more powerful Pondo tribe.

Once more, but this time in Mount Ayliff, we had the good fortune to be assisted by a young man whose family had lived and traded in the district for three generations. He drove us in his own vehicle which had a high clearance, up a rough track into the mountains where we discovered people whose dress and beadwork we had not known existed. The Xesibe tribe still scarify their faces and probably in consequence of the many vicissitudes they have passed through, employ more facial scarification marks than any other tribe in the Transkei. The whole face — forehead, nose, cheeks and chin bear a mass of long thin scar lines — the indelible marks of their tribe.

The women grow their hair. They smear it with fat and ochre and plait it into many thin chains that hang shoulder-length, or they plait thicker chains which are interwoven with coloured wool or thread and these hang loosely down the back. They decorate the ends with attractive loops of beads. They favour bright green and orange-red wool and these colours are repeated in their beadwork. They do not use ochre on their clothing but smear on pork fat or vaseline; later the cloth turns a brownish-black colour. In place of the brass wire employed by most other tribes the Xesibes use an aluminium wire to make their arm bands, leg bands and waist bands. The aluminium tones in very well with the colour of their clothing. All married women wear a narrow beaded head ring often held in position by a snuff spoon. When they have a baby they take off the pretty head ring and wear a plain ring made of plaited thread. They wear slim skirts slit up the side and edged in white beads. In build they are small boned and they have slanted eyes which give their faces a slightly oriental appearance.

For parties and festivals the teenagers wear spectacular bead-dress. They combine it with small jingling bells, showy pompoms of green and orange wool and ornaments made of aluminium wire. Both sexes wear beaded head bands and beaded ear-rings decorated with rakish wool pompoms. As is usual in tribal custom each girl makes her boy friend's beadwork, and among the Xesibes this is no mean feat. A well-dressed young man wears an elaborate head-dress, beaded arm bands, a fine bead collar and a black skirt covered with rows of beaded tags each in a different motif — a taxingly intricate method of bead embroidery. All beadwork is essentially decorative but the Xesibe women achieve magnificent results.

CHAPTER VII

THE FINGO TRIBE

*T*he 'Fingo' tribe have had an extremely varied history. Not only were they broken through defeat and dismemberment by the Zulus but subsequently they were moved in and about the Transkei and Ciskei. The Xhosa term amaMfengu has become Fingo in European usage. 'Fingo' is properly Mfengu — a wanderer, displaced person or beggar. The term was applied collectively to certain refugees from Natal. In the terrible wars of Shaka, the Hlubi tribe crossed the Drakensberg and sought refuge in Basutoland but other members of this tribe together with the Zizi and Bhele tribes fled southwards and entered Tembu and Gcaleka territory. The survivors were destitute, helpless and so stricken by famine that they had resorted to eating grass and to cannibalism. They wore clothing made from grass. When asked 'Who are you?', they replied *Siyamfenguza* — 'We are destitute' or 'We seek service'. Many settled in Tembuland where they were kindly received and like many broken tribes placed under their own chiefs.

The majority settled in Gcalekaland where Hintsa, chief of the Gcaleka, employed them as hut builders, herdsmen and milkers. Their wage was the milk of the cows lent to them for that purpose. They took the greatest care of the cows and calves and in order to keep them in good condition chose those parts of the country with the most abundant grass. They also used the grass to make mats and baskets. In their poverty, the Fingos carefully preserved their clan names, and cherished the hope of freedom, their own country and cattle. Under Hintsa the Gcalekas began to oppress the Fingos but Soga* states that they were never actually enslaved. On their arrival in 1828 they had been befriended by the Reverend Ayliff of the Wesleyan Mission at Butterworth. In 1835 on representation by the Fingos, he petitioned the Governor of the Cape, Sir Benjamin D'Urban, who was on a visit to Butterworth, to take them under British protection. The Governor agreed and arranged to resettle them in the Ciskei at Peddie, between the Keiskama and Great Fish rivers. Unfortunately the term 'emancipation' was applied to the exodus of the Fingos from Gcalekaland. It must be recalled that the Fingos had arrived as paupers and yet seven years later, in 1835, they left as rich men! When the famous Fingo migration began the column that left Butterworth was 2½ km wide and 12 km long. In company with the Governor and Ayliff, their missionary, they crossed the Kei River and they numbered over 17 000 persons in possession of 15 000 cattle. Furthermore many thousands of Fingos had chosen to remain in Gcalekaland where they were accepted as British subjects.

* Soga, J.H.: *The South-Eastern Bantu*

Subsequently in 1865, the Fingos who had remained were settled by Governor Philip Wodehouse in the central part of the Transkei between the Kei and Bashee rivers, in the districts of Butterworth, Nqamakwe and Tsomo. The territory was called Fingoland. Before the cattle killing the Gcalekas had lived in this territory and, therefore, the proud Gcaleka Chief, Kreli, and his people resented the occupation of a portion of their ancestral land. It led to quarrels and later to a war in which the British assisted the Fingos and the Gcalekas were defeated.

It is remarkable that despite their history of hardship and close contact with their hosts, the Tembu and Gcaleka tribes, the Fingos nevertheless have survived as a separate tribal unit. Although they have assimilated the customs and dress of the Xhosa they are still renowned for the delicate workmanship of their grasswork, and their dress and beadwork show a fine sense of colour that is distinct from that of the Tembu or Gcaleka.

In the old days the tribe favoured pink and blue beads. They used more pink beads than any other tribe in the Transkei, for these shades of pink contrasted favourably with their brown-red ochred clothing. Among the older generation a dark blue and pink necklace is still popular for a deep collar. Formerly the Fingo women and girls decorated their shawls and skirts with many rows of buttons. There was no set design, only straight rows of small white buttons, sometimes twenty rows requiring more than a thousand buttons. But unlike the London Costers they refused pearl buttons and only used white china buttons. Owens in his diary (1836) mentions that the natives were paid with buttons. Since the last war china buttons have been unobtainable and pearl buttons have been substituted but not as many are used. In recent years the price of buttons and beads has risen so enormously that they are becoming an increasingly rare commodity.

The districts of Butterworth, Nqamakwe and Tsomo have remained predominantly Fingo but Fingo clans are also to be found in Tembuland and smaller units are scattered throughout the Transkei. The tribe was deeply grateful for the assistance given to them by the missionaries and throughout Fingoland mission institutions and schools have flourished with the result that today little or no tribal life is to be seen. There are isolated pockets but it was with the utmost difficulty that one was found. Repeatedly I called upon old traders in what used to be traditional Fingo territory only to be told that the tribal dress and beadwork had disappeared. Eventually a Fingo settlement was located near the confluence of the Bashee and Xuka rivers, in isolated and extremely rugged terrain. There was no school, no trading store and also no road.

We chose to visit the area at the weekend. We travelled on a rough earth road to a small native village where I ascertained that the Fingo clan lived further afield and a distant hill was indicated. I asked if there was a road and my informant airily replied 'Oh yes, there's the road'. We went down a rapidly disintegrating track. We rocketed from pothole to pothole. I do not know how the springs stood up or why we did not have a puncture. We reached another settlement where our arrival aroused considerable interest. The track wound through valleys and past steep hills covered with large rocks. It was often hair-raising. We had to stop and I had to get out again and again to navigate a passage between the boulders. Startled goats leapt delicately from rock to rock and gazed at us enquiringly.

But when we arrived there was never a dull moment. Not only was it a Fingo settlement but they were *en fête*. The previous day three young men had completed their three-month period of isolation and initiation and had graduated to full manhood. A great party called *umgidi* had been arranged to welcome them. In such a remote area social life is all important. All participate and all doors stand open. All night there had been dancing, feasting and drinking. No one had slept. The older people were still enjoying the beer. Every one was in full tribal dress for this is what their life and living were all about — a handing on of the glory of their past heritage. This was the gift of the community to the new men of their tribe. It was a day of tremendous significance and importance, a day to be savoured slowly and to the full.

The newly initiated young men are known as *amakrwala* and they were quite easily recognisable. Their faces were painted with ochre and each wore a neat black cashmere doek tied low on the forehead. Most prominent among their insignia of graduation to manhood were two necklaces, a choker of dog's teeth and a neck band of black otter or water-vole fur, both being necklaces of great symbolic significance. Each was resplendent in a blue blanket covered by a brightly coloured rug. The other young men of this age group wore three blankets — an orange and a Fingo brown-red surmounted by a white woollen blanket. Each blanket was edged with at least four rows of pearl buttons. They wore full tribal dress and enormous hoop ear-rings. All wore their clothes with elegance and ease.

The young women of this age group wore short brown-red skirts decorated with green, white and orange beads, and rows of pearl buttons. In front of the skirt, like a sporran, they wore a small cloth tobacco bag, heavily beaded and fringed with leather thongs and each carried a cow's tail set in a beaded handle. They wore masses of brass arm bands, leg bands and a great quantity of beadwork. Their faces were painted with yellow ochre and their lips outlined in black, and two black marks were painted on their cheeks. Both the men and the women were well built and showed a physique reminiscent of their distant Zulu ancestry.

We spent the day with the tribe and in the unspoilt simplicity of the surrounding terrain we savoured the charm of an archaic culture, a culture that strikes a balance between man and his natural environment, of man made by his society, illuminating the influence each has upon the other.

Alice took the last photograph and our tribal mosaic was complete. Gcaleka, Tembu, Pondo, Bomvana, Mpondomise, Xesibe, Bhaca and Fingo, and what a delightful mosaic they had made. Our journey was over and we had a treasure chest of photographs and memories. Photographs that attest to a culture essentially rich in human qualities — not an alien culture but part of the great heritage of man.

Life around the kraal

Wherever one looks one sees the kraals. They are spread far and wide — beside the sea, on the hills overlooking the sea, in the plains, in the valleys, on the mountain tops and near the great forests. Most kraal owners possess a few cattle, sheep and goats, one or two pigs, and several fowls. During the spring the men plough the fields. When the maize or sorghum is well established they employ a light cultivator drawn by two oxen to loosen the soil between the rows of plants. Thereafter it is the women's duty to hoe the lands and the men concern themselves with building, thatching and tending the cattle.

In tribal life the distribution of work falls unfairly upon the women. In the kraals there is segregation of the sexes from an early age. In the huts the girls and women are required to sit on one side and the men and the boys on the opposite side. From the age of five years boys are taught to associate with the males of the family and to share the manly tasks.

Boys of ten to sixteen years tend the cattle and milk the cows while their younger brothers of five to ten years tend the sheep, goats and calves. The youngest boys look after the lambs. If a lamb becomes separated from its mother and loses its way a small boy of five places it across his shoulders and carries it safely home. Every morning the shepherds, accompanied by their dogs, drive their herds and flocks to the grazing lands. Each boy carries a stick with which he admonishes his charges, driving them with shrill calls and birdlike whistles. The boys also use their sticks to fence, an art in which they become most proficient.

From the age of five years the girls are taught to assist their mothers. They help to tend the baby, cook, clean, sweep, fetch firewood and water. The last two chores occupy many hours, for water must be fetched daily and it is not uncommon for a woman to walk two to three kilometres to draw a bucket of water. Fuel is equally hard to come by for kraal owners seldom if ever plant trees. Therefore once or twice a week a woman must walk to the nearest plantation to gather a head-load of wood. When firewood is unprocurable, cow dung is collected and burnt. It gives off an unforgettable aromatic smell, a tang that is an inseparable element of the Transkei air. The soft greyness of its smoke is very beautiful, especially as it uncurls over the huts, drifts into the valleys and creeps up the mountain sides.

The staple diet of the people is maize, supplemented by kaffir beer. The women and girls stamp the maize in handmade blocks and then winnow the grain. They cook in three-legged pots on open fires in front of the huts. On most days there is a pot of boiled maize for the family, but in summertime when milk is plentiful mealie meal is served mixed with curdled milk — a delicious traditional dish.

Beer is brewed regularly. Maize is used, and the women and girls grind it on a hollowed stone. Water is added to the meal which is allowed to ferment, and then the gruel is boiled. For beer-drinks and parties beer is brewed in tremendous quantities. This necessitates the borrowing of pots and barrels from friends and neighbours who are always willing to oblige.

In addition to washing the family's blankets and clothing, the women and girls plaster and colour-wash the huts, and gather food from the lands. These activities are looked upon as daily chores but they are followed by the more favoured occupations of grasswork, beadwork, making new clothes, dressing up in beads, preparing for dances, painting their faces and those of their children, and decorating the body or face with the tribal scarification marks. All are skills that are passed from mother to daughter. Grandmothers and mothers are careful to uphold tribal traditions, and the grandmothers play an especially important role. Every night the children cluster around the grandmother and listen to tribal stories. She teaches them to sing, to clap the rhythm of the songs and to practise the tribal dance steps.

From every kraal a network of footpaths is to be seen. These lead to the fields, to the river or stream, to the grazing lands and to the trading store. All are used daily. The trading store is the centre of activity. The women and girls do most of the shopping, but when bags of maize, meal or fertilizer are required the men supervise the loading of the sleighs and the transportation.

The men enjoy a far easier life. They have endless time for lengthy conversations on community affairs, family celebrations, the choosing of animals for sacrifice, and quite often they enjoy a day's hunting. Most kraal owners possess two or more whippet-like dogs which have great speed and are most successful in hunting jackals, wild cats, buck and hares. In Gcalekaland we met a delightful old man who posed with his two hunting dogs. The dogs were decorated with necklaces made from the skin of their quarry.

2

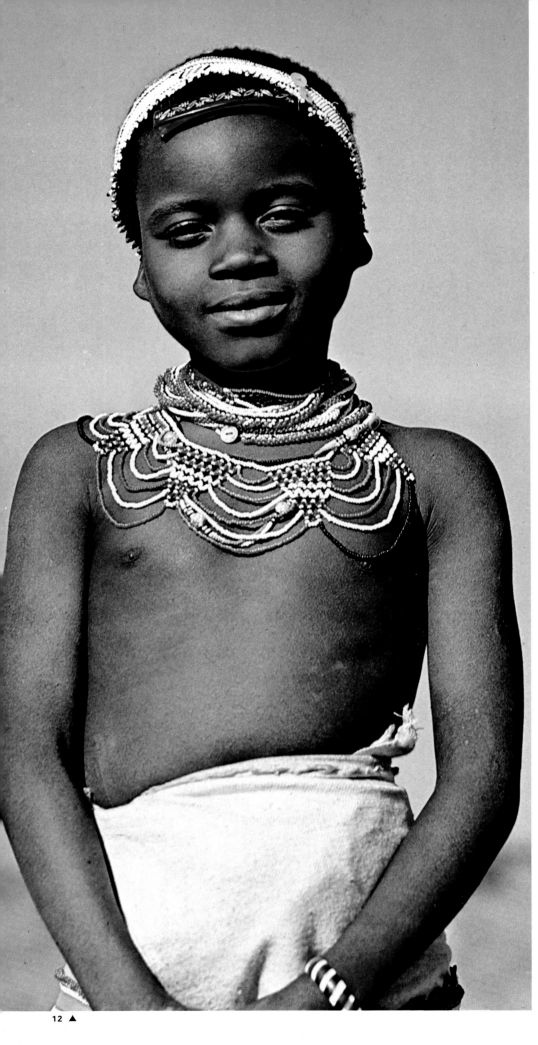

12 ▲

13 ▲

14 ▲

15 ▼

16 ▲

17 ▲

► 18

21 ▲   22 ▲   23 ▼

25

26

27

28

35

36

43 ▲

◄
42

◄
44

46 ▲

47 ▲

45 ▲

48 ▲

50 ▼   49 ▲

51 ▼

52 ▲ 53 ▼ 54 ▼

55 ▲   56 ▼   57 ▼   58 ▼

59 ▲

60 ▲

61 ▼

62 ▲

63 ▼

64 ▼

65 ▲

66 ▲

67 ▼

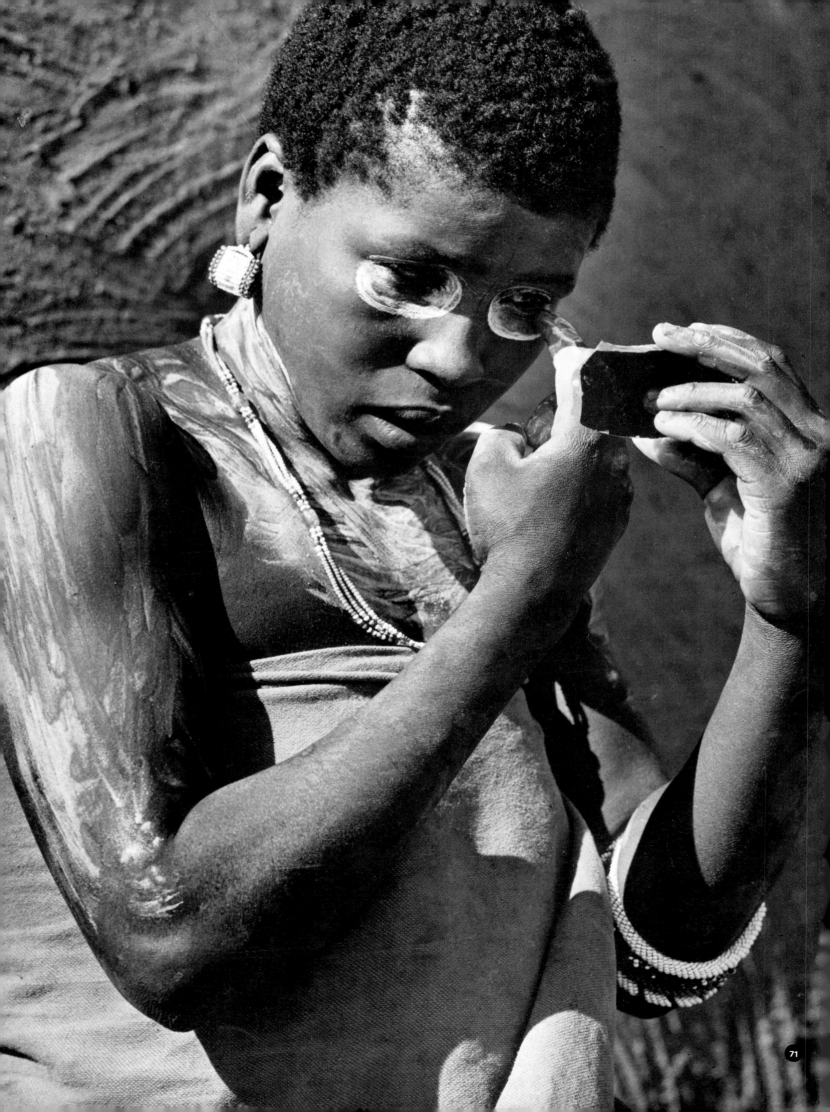

The seven faces of the Transkei

Within the Transkei there are eleven main tribes. Seven of these figure prominently in the photographs that follow. Although the language spoken is Xhosa, the tribes are distinct in area, tribal dress, personality, and physical type. There is also a slight variation in skin colouring, from darker brown to the lighter shades. Real beauty is a matter of bone formation and natural colouring, but in each tribe nature is assisted by painting ochre or clay on the face to enhance attractive features and to hide others. Patterns are also made by scarification, and paint and ochre are used on the body and clothing. The tribal conceptions of beauty vary, but each captures the imagination.

The Tembus are the oldest tribe in the Transkei and therefore it was common for neighbouring chiefs to seek new wives in Tembuland. As a result the word for polygamy in Xhosa is *isithembu*. The Tembu women are not the most beautiful, but it has always seemed to me that they hold their heads higher and smile more confidently than the women of other tribes.

In the early days the Tembus practised a form of mutilation of the body whereby the first joint of the little finger was removed. The custom was not observed by the tribe as a whole but was and still is performed in infancy or early childhood in cases of ill-health where it is believed to appease the ancestral spirits. This practice is also found but to a lesser extent in the Fingo and Gcaleka tribes.

The Tembus do not scarify their faces, but from puberty the girls are scarified from the navel in three lines between the breasts, and in diagonal lines above and below the breasts, thus enhancing their beauty. For social gatherings the girls and young women paint their faces in intricate patterns of white clay which they apply with a fine stick or quill.

When they attend important functions, or when they dance, the women cover their arms and the upper parts of their bodies with yellow ochre which imparts an attractive appearance and a silky feel. The Tembu women favour massive head-dresses in a great diversity of styles, each being a unique creation.

The Gcaleka women are tall and distinguished-looking. They have fine features which convey an expression of extraordinary beauty. The girls are very pretty and have lovely slim bodies. Their skins gleam with a satin smoothness and their breasts are firm and provocative. Facial scarification is not employed, but shoulders and arms are scarified, drawing attention to the suppleness of their backs. For dances the women cover their arms and upper torso with red ochre and paint their faces in designs of yellow or white ochre.

The Pondo are smaller in build and darker in skin colour. They establish their individuality by facial scarification, duck-egg blue blankets, and long hair. In adolescence the little twists of hair are laid flat against the head with a fringe on the forehead. But later on the young men and women plait this fringe and roll it in soft wire so that it stands in one long curl above the forehead or nose. Another much-admired characteristic among the Pondo is the gap between the two upper incisors. Called *umhlantla* it is looked upon as a sign of great beauty and is used to spit through.

Of the remaining tribes, those of the Bomvana, Xesibe, Mpondomise and Fingo, each has its particular characteristics and aids to beauty. These are to be seen in facial features, shades of ochre, scarification marks, beadwork and clothing — all of which have been described in the text. The people have a distinctive elegance and each tribe's artistic instinct expresses the essence of African beauty.

81

82

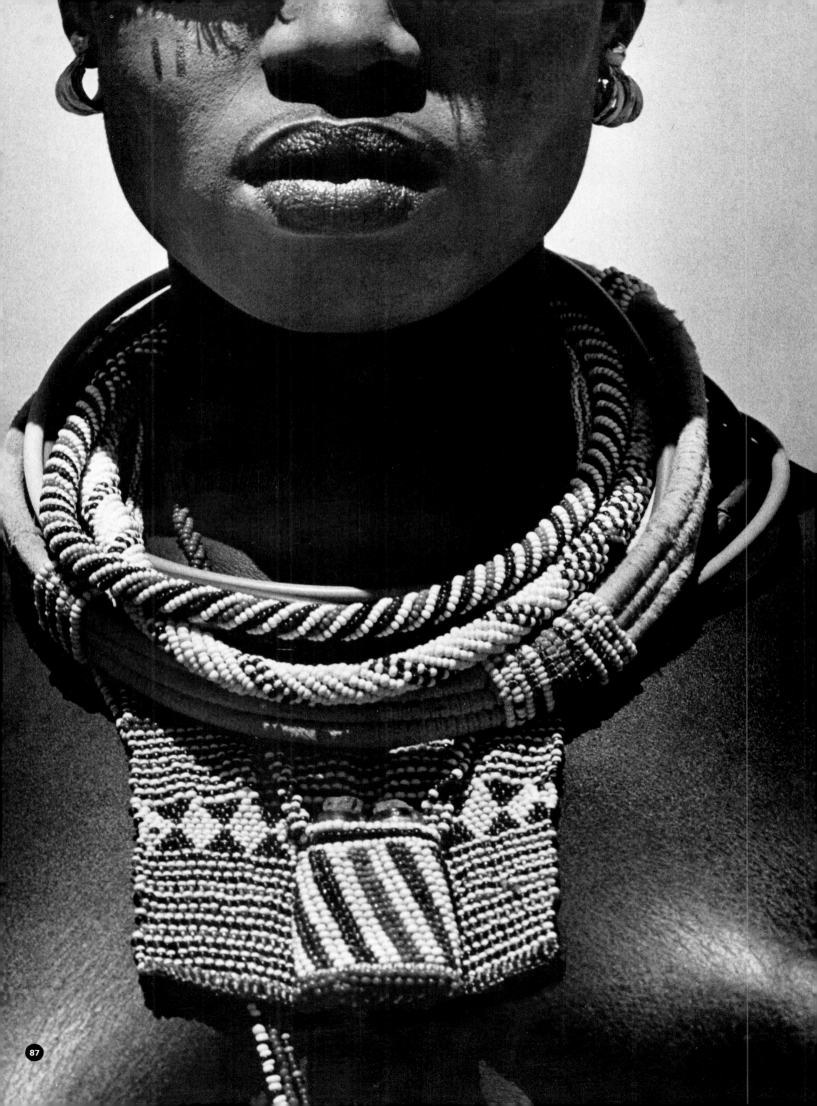

99 ▲

100 ▲   101 ▼

◄
98

102 ▲   103 ▼   104 ▼   105 ▼

The witchdoctors

In the old days the tribes were held in thrall to witchcraft. Not only did the chiefs believe implicitly in the witchdoctors, but they actively supported them. Those whom the witchdoctors 'smelt out', men and women alike, were put to death by means of the most barbaric cruelty. 'Smelling out' was forbidden by the Cape Government and punishable by law and therefore the practice gradually died out in all tribes except the Pondo. The Pondos were the last independent tribe and one of their chiefs, Umhlangaso, strove to the utmost of his power against annexation but eventually in 1894 the chiefs signed the agreement. ·

Until this time witchcraft was rife in Pondoland and it is said that no less than five persons per week were accused of sorcery and put to death. One of the less cruel methods, comparatively speaking, was to drive the victims to an execution rock from which they were flung down. The last of these executions took place within living memory, at a high krantz overlooking the Umzimvubu River. It is called execution rock and is to be seen on the road to Majola. The victims were chased with assegais up the easy approach to the krantz and forced to jump over the cataclysmic cliff, their bones splintering on the rocks below.

In every tribe the power of the witchdoctor was supreme. This is clearly illustrated in the terrible cattle-killing delusion which in 1857 almost annihilated the Gcaleka tribe of whom Kreli was Chief. The tribal witchdoctor, Mhlakaza, lived on the Gxara River in the Kentani district. His fifteen-year-old niece Nongqause was in her novitiate training to be his acolyte. On the Gxara River there was a pool of water close to the sea and as the tide rose the water in the pool was disturbed by the incoming tide. It was and still is a beautiful pool, shaded by palms, wild bananas and other trees. The pool was near Mhlakaza's kraal and Nongqause used to sit on a rock in the pool and gaze into the water where she saw her ancestral spirits. They told her to tell the chief to order his people to kill all their animals, to empty their grain-pits and to scatter the food until the land be obscured by the chaff driven by the wind. Once these instructions had been fulfilled all the animals would come alive again and all the Gcalekas who had died would come alive. The land would fill with people and with sleek cattle and the grain-pits would be filled to overflowing. Then the departed chiefs would arise and lead their people forth into a great battle against the whites who would be driven into the sea from whence they had come.

Mhlakaza told Kreli of the visions and forthwith the chief proclaimed and espoused the prophecies of the powerful enchantress Nongqause. He urged the Gcaleka and other tribes to destroy all their stock and grain in one sublime act of dedication to the ancestral spirits. All the tribal people believed in dreams but this was a dream of disaster and all were not unanimously agreed. Kreli considered himself Paramount Chief of the whole Xhosa nation but more than a hundred years previously a quarrel had led to a split in the nation and the Rarabes (also known as Gaikas) who were descended from the right-hand house had cut themselves off from the great house and had crossed the Kei River and settled in the Ciskei where Lord Charles Somerset had appointed Gaika as Paramount Chief over them. His son Sandile now ruled. Kreli called on him to join in the cattle-killing but fortunately the Gaika Commissioner, Charles Brownlee, exercised his influence upon Sandile.

But betrayed by the false prophecy of Nongqause the Gcalekas obeyed Kreli and two-thirds of the tribe, an estimated 70 000, perished in a frenzy of starvation. Words fail to describe the depth of this holocaust whereby a living tribe destroyed itself.

One Sunday Alice and I drove to the Gxara River in order to photograph Nongqause's pool, but en route we lost our way. We stopped at a church to make enquiries and the African Minister very kindly introduced us to a man whose father owned the land next to Nongqause's pool. His name was Lenteni and he offered to accompany us. He was a charming man, friendly and courteous, and we thoroughly enjoyed his company. His presence with us at the pool made a deep impression. The pool represented Nongqause, a Gcaleka of 1857 while Lenteni with his talk of night-schools for African adults, represented a Gcaleka of today.

Among the tribes of the Transkei the beat of the witchdoctor's drum is still heard. Although they practise their magic which to the uneducated is charged with meaning and infinite possibilities, nevertheless their tremendous hold has been broken. Many of the witchdoctors tend to be unapproachable and sometimes the expression on their faces is stiff, saturnine and menacing, whereas their counterparts, the witchdoctresses, are much more approachable and appear an easier and happier breed.

The abakhwetha
INITIATION INTO MANHOOD

The Gcaleka, Tembu, Fingo, Bomvana and Mpondomise tribes observe the custom of circumcision. It is used to mark entrance into manhood and is regarded as the most solemn occasion in the life of every man. The approved age is about nineteen or twenty years. For two months or more after circumcision the initiates, known as *abakhwetha,* live in isolation in a specially constructed grass hut or lodge. It is usually built in a secluded area where they enjoy complete privacy, for during this period no women may look upon their faces. An instructor looks after the initiates and a small errand boy also lives at the lodge.

The operation of circumcision is performed by a skilled tribesman but his methods of surgery and hygiene are primitive. For the first week the *abakhwetha* remain in their lodge and are treated by their nurse-instructor. By the eighth day their wounds have healed and each initiate smears his entire body with white clay and is free to roam in the veld. White clay covering the face, body and clothing indicates contact with the ancestral spirits and shows that the wearer is in a state of transition and excluded from normal tribal life. The religious significance of the custom of circumcision is further emphasised by three propitiatory sacrifices. The first is made just before the operation, the second is made on the healing of the wounds and the third when the initiates graduate. In the old days before they 'came out' the *abakhwetha* performed the spectacular *umtshilo* dances in specially designed palm-leaf skirts and head-dresses. But the custom has slowly died out in all tribes except the Gcaleka. Here too there has been no *umtshilo* dancing since the death of the chief, for his wife, the regent, requested that as a sign of mourning the tribe forego the practise although it is slowly being revived.

I had arranged our first visit to Gcalekaland to coincide with the harvesting of the crops, my express purpose being to obtain pictures of initiation ceremonies. The latter had commenced and several lodges were to be seen. Again we were given assistance by an old trading family. Their son drove us in his jeep to visit the fathers of initiates. The purpose of our book was explained to them and one of them accompanied us to his son's lodge. The trader was a close friend of these *abakhwetha.* He spoke to them and asked them to allow Alice to take photographs of them. This lodge held six but we saw only two men. The one was not feeling well and his friend had remained to keep him company while the other four had gone hunting. Both agreed to be photographed but the one called Mpondo looked drawn and ill. His condition was more serious than we realised for a week later we were shocked to hear of his death which we presumed was caused by septicaemia.

Rumours of *umtshilo* dances were rife but no definite information was available. Eventually Noyonk' offered to walk many miles to a kraal which was reported to be holding an *umtshilo.* It was a long journey for an old woman and she returned weary but with the good news that the beer barrels were being washed out and that the dance would be held on the eighth day. Luck was with us for not only was there to be an *umtshilo* but two days before the dance the *abakhwetha* were to hold a full dress rehearsal and we made arrangements to attend both performances.

For an *umtshilo* dance each initiate wears a palm-leaf skirt and head-dress. The costumes are made by a special man who selects the young shoots of the wild palm before the leaves have opened and are still tender. These are pulled off the stem and threaded with fine string and hung in the sun to dry. They bleach white. Each skirt consists of six metres of threaded leaves. These are wound around the initiate's waist where they stand out in a skirt far fuller than that of a ballerina's tutu. The *abakhwetha* may not dance in public unless masked so a huge head-dress of dried palm leaves is tied to the head where, although it entirely covers the face, it allows limited vision through the interstices. To each head-dress is affixed a long palm stem crowned with a black feather or one or two leaves. Part of the dancing is to make this stem fall forward to touch the ground as gracefully as possible. In his right hand the initiate holds an assegai and his left wrist is decorated with a black horse-tail.

In order to attend the rehearsal we had to follow the footpaths. Loaded with cameras we waded through two rivers, then ascended a steep hill. The lodge had been built midway on the hillside and when we arrived the crowd had already gathered. On the hilltop sat sixteen women beating a staked cow hide and chanting. Below them were groups of women, teenagers and children. Next sat rows of older men with the younger men sitting in front of them. All faced the lodge. Also present as spectators were *abakhwetha* from neighbouring lodges. We watched enthralled as a small boy led in a line of these men. They walked in single file. Each had his face completely covered by his blanket and all that showed was the palm-leaf crest that decorated his head.

As the initiates filed out of their lodge to commence the rehearsal the women chanted triumphantly:—

> *Hail, Hail,*
> *Here are our* abakhwetha,
> *Here are our new men,*
> *Observe their white clay,*
> *Look upon the feather of the black crow*
> *And the tail of the black horse.*

The *abakhwetha* danced with knees bent and arms outstretched, assegais raised and horse-tails quivering. Throughout their performance the older men called out encouragement or insults. 'What! These are a bunch of women! Come on, Zwelikumbi, show your father's blood! Make the palm leaves rattle! Shake them! Dance!'

If his skirt or mask slipped the initiate immediately raised his right hand across his face and the younger men rushed forward with blankets outstretched to shield him while the fault was rectified. As they danced the *abakhwetha* made a high keening cry. Sometimes they made as if they would throw an assegai or would take aim as if to shoot, and then like ballet dancers they mimed death, panting in terrible agony like beings mortally wounded. At one stage of the rehearsal the instructor led them. Dancing most beautifully he showed them how to glide smoothly with waltzing steps — forwards, backwards, pirouette, hesitate, bend the body far forward and rattle the back of the skirt, then bend backwards and rattle the front of the skirt.

Within two days the *abakhwetha* were fully proficient and ready to present their exhibition dance. Their dress was the same but superimposed on the white clay had been painted geometrical patterns of blue and red dots and streaks — primitive symbols representing the leopard, the national emblem of the Gcaleka tribe. At the kraal a great concourse had gathered. As the initiates filed out of the cattle-fold they were greeted by the rhythmic chanting of the praise-names of their families with particular allusion to the father of each initiate. This show of pride created a splendid feeling of atmosphere and in a mood of exultation each man gave an impeccable performance of unique beauty. Charged with meaning their dance completed the tribal link and was their 'thank you' to the ancestral spirits for bringing them to manhood. It was an exciting and memorable occasion. Pride shone in the faces of fathers, mothers, brothers and sisters, all of whom shared and cherished every moment of the proceedings.

127 ▲

126 ▲

128 ▲   129 ▼

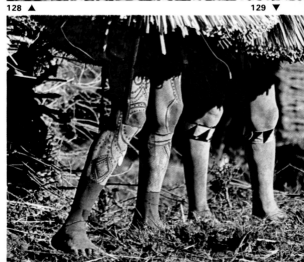

131 ▲ 132 ▼ 133 ▼ 134 ▼

The tribal dances

In all tribes that practise circumcision the dances are arranged in age groups that fall into four main categories. These being those for teenagers, those for young adults, those for married women and those for the older men. Each creates a glamorous impression and succeeds in imparting skill, beauty and grace to tribal life.

The teenagers organise a dance called an *umtshotsho*. It is usually held once a week and is the tribal gathering for all adolescents. A girl attends until her eighteenth year and a youth attends until he is circumcised. The *umtshotsho* is planned and controlled entirely by teenagers and is administered by a committee of senior youths. Each location holds its own *umtshotsho*. The teenagers gather at sunset and dance throughout the night. They return home towards midday.

At Mazeppa Bay the *umtshotsho* is held every Thursday night and so our best time to take photographs was upon a Friday morning. The girls are pretty, have lovely slim bodies and their firm strong breasts are always exposed. Dancing, courtship and beadwork are intimately woven into the social structure. The girls make beadwork for their boy friends to wear and all dress up for the dance. In Tembuland we met, and Alice photographed, a particularly beautiful teenage couple. The girl had the blossoming beauty and melting quality of a young Juliet.

The traditional tribal dance for young adults is called the *intlombe* It is attended by all young men and women of marriageable age. No man may join until he has been circumcised and once a girl marries she is debarred from the dance. The *intlombe* is held once or twice a month on a Saturday night. It is usual for each location to hold an *intlombe* but occasionally they combine. In Gcalekaland we had the good fortune to attend a magnificent dance in which several locations had joined. We would not have gained admittance had it not been for Mr Revu, a member of the Transkeian Legislative Assembly. He arranged the invitation and escorted us. The beadwork, dress and dancing were superb. The men carried a beautifully beaded bifid stick and danced in front of the women. The latter were pretty, gay and romantic. They wore long skirts and magnificent turbans and being unmarried they danced with their breasts exposed.

The *intlombe* is followed in time-honoured sequence by the dance of the older men. Its membership is restricted to an age group from over thirty to late middle age. The dance is held once a month. Each location has its own organisation but usually the locations combine and hold a grand dance lasting two to three days. Although the dance is for married men their wives do not attend except as spectators. The men dance with their mistresses and a class of women known as *amadikazi*. The latter include widows, divorcées and wives deserted by their husbands. Thus the older men's dance gives these women a special place in the social structure of the tribe and allows them to enjoy the pleasures of community life. Although the women tend to dress flamboyantly the men are very elegant. In Tembuland we met a group of unusually handsome and well-dressed men whose dignity, poise and self-assurance were most impressive.

The dance for the married women is known as the *umngqungqo* and is always performed at the initiation of a girl into womanhood. In Emigrant Tembuland we attended one of these dances, and were enthralled by the beauty of the tribal dress and beadwork. On the morning of the *umngqungqo* a large barrel of beer is placed between the cattle-fold and the huts and from midday until sunset the women circle the beer barrel. Sticks held aloft they sing and dance, and in tribal tradition present a pageant of beauty. Then as the setting sun casts its golden aura, and the smoke uncurls over the huts, the sound of their singing dies away and the women wend their way homeward.

149

154 ▲

155 ▲

◄ 156

158 ▲ 159 ▲ 160 ▲ 161 ▼